FOLK &
FIGURE
WOOD
CARVING

17 Detailed Patterns with Full Color Photos
plus a Step-by-Step Carving Project

by Ross Oar

S0-AZO-813

Copyright © 1999 Fox Chapel Publishing Company Inc. The patterns contained herein are copyrighted by the author. Artists may make any number of projects based on these patterns. The patterns themselves, however, are not to be photocopied for resale or distribution under any circumstances. Any such copying is a violation of copyright laws.

Publisher: Alan Giagnocavo
Project Editor: Ayleen Stellhorn
Desktop Specialist: Linda L. Eberly, Eberly Designs Inc.
Interior Photography: Bob Polett
Cover Photography: Bob Polett

ISBN # 1-56523-105-8

To order your copy of this book,
please send check or money order
for $14.95 plus $2.50 shipping to:
Fox Books Orders
1970 Broad Street
East Petersburg, PA 17520

───────── *D e d i c a t i o n* ─────────

I would like to thank Alan Giagnocavo for his encouragement in my carving book endeavors and, as always, my wife Barbara.

To write the author or to inquire about rough-outs, send a self-addressed stamped envelope to:

Ross Oar
West Falls Woodcarving
7458 Ellicott Road
West Falls, NY 14170
(716) 662-3648

Contents

Ross Oar has had many years of experience in woodcarving. In 1984, he and his wife, Barbara, began West Falls Woodcarving, a part-time mail-order woodcarving supplies business run out of their home in Orchard Park, New York. Ross also carves commission pieces that range in size from three inches to five and a half feet high and depict all aspects of life, teaches woodcarving classes on a limited basis and participates in woodcarving shows.

Ross has worked in various forms of art since childhood. His mother, an art school graduate, and his father, an antique dealer and metal craftsman, gave him the necessary support and guidance to design and create while he was young. Over the years he has done many interesting commissions from illustrating children's books to carving for churches. Other skills include metal casting, forging, engraving, pattern making, printing and self-publishing. Black powder gunmaking, leather work, bead work and scrimshaw art, which are part of early American history, have been rewarding challenges.

Ross is the author of *Christmas Heirloom Patterns Volumes I and II* and inventor of the Oar Sharpener and other patents. His wife, Barbara, is his biggest support and always helps with new endeavors.

The Knife
An ancient tool more beneficial than a jewel
performed many a duel, this nobel tool.
Always useful this handy tool.
Defending all the world.
Providing food, shelter and carvings in wood.
Though many types and variations have been made,
it still remains a knife and a nobel tool.
What would a woodcarver do without this tool
The knife

–Ross Oar

Woodcarving is one of the oldest art forms in the world, dating back to the use of ancient tribal totem poles and dolls. I also find it to be one of the most enjoyable art forms. I am thrilled again and again with the feeling of accomplishment after I finish each new project. Many others I have met over the years have shown the same enthusiasm for woodcarving.

Getting started as a woodcarver is not very difficult. I have created this book to interest and challenge you, whether you are a beginning carver or an experienced carver. You can alter the patterns found on the pages of this book to create simpler or more complex carvings, use the ideas to create your own designs or follow the patterns provided. Just remember: Do not become discouraged the first time you attempt to carve. Everyone can improve his or her woodcarving skills with experimentation and practice. You need to develop your own woodcarving techniques as you carve. Over the years, I have found woodcarving to be very relaxing and helpful in relieving stress. I hope you will also.

In order to best depict the techniques common in woodcarving I have chosen a variety of subjects for this book. The range of difficulty will change throughout the book. Pick the pattern you are most comfortable with and then gradually move into the more difficult projects. The projects titled *Toothache* and *Santa Relief* are good projects for beginning woodcarvers.

A more advanced carver will still find the projects in this book challenging, yet he will perhaps want to stray from the pattern at times and experiment. When possible, I try to show added and more advanced features. Not only will this keep the advanced carver interested, but it will enable the beginner to return to earlier works and refine them once his or her skill level improves.

Also in this book, I have included a step-by-step project, "Carving a Female Face". I chose to demonstrate carving the female face because I believe it to be more difficult than carving the male face. In talking with other carvers, they always express difficulty with women's and children's faces.

The most important rule in woodcarving is to relax and have fun. Do not be frustrated if your end product is not an exact replica of your pattern. Mistakes will help you learn for your next carving and may even make for a better piece. So go get your wood, your tools and sit back and enjoy yourself.

Selecting Tools

When selecting tools, start out with only the basics. The tools that I use have been collected over years of carving. A carving can be done with just a knife; however, gouges and special tools can make the project easier and add more character and detail to a carving.

Tools in my toolbox:
- knife with steel of 59–60 Rockwell (I favor Helvie Knives and Notto Knives.)
- X-acto® style knife or one with a very thin blade
- Oar Sharpener for holding consistent angles on your carving gouges, v's and chisels
- coarse and fine sharpening stones
- buffing rouge and leather strop (I also use scrap pieces of basswood with rouge to hone)
- 1mm, 1/8", 3/16", 1/4", 3/8", 1/2", 5/8", number 9 or 10 gouges
- #10mm V-tool 75%, Micro V

Pictured is my traveling tool box.

A sharp tool is necessary to produce a successful woodcarving. A tool can be checked for sharpness by touching your fingernail to the blade, sharp edge down, and scraping the sharp edge lightly across your nail. (You can also try this on a block of wood.) If the blade drags, your tool is sharp. If not, keep sharpening it until it drags. The one thing I see every time I teach a class is dull tools. Keeping your tools sharp is the most important part of carving.

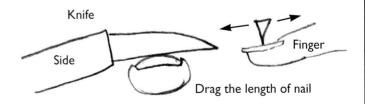

Learn to sharpen your tools and see the positive results.

Don't let your tools become blunt. A tool can be sharp and still be what I call blunt. You should use a sharpening stone occasionally to keep your tools at the proper angle. Angles may vary depending on your personal preferences. Most are between 16° and 20°. I have designed a hand sharpening guide jig for sharpening and keeping the proper angles on your gouges, v-tools, chisels and skews. The Oar Sharpener is available through West Falls Woodcarving (see our address in the front of the book).

For sharpening gouges, V tools, chisels and skews, I have developed a jig to maintain constant angles. The Oar Sharpener is shown here.

Choosing Wood

Most professional carvers use basswood, and for the projects in this book, basswood is my choice. However, there are many more types of wood to use, depending on what is available and what the carver wants to create. If great detail is desired, I use basswood or tupelo. If you want to create a carving with a natural wood color, butternut, black walnut and cherry are good choices. The following woods are rated as I see them in order of carving ease, with 1 being the easiest and 10 being the hardest.

1 Basswood
2 Tupelo
3 Butternut
4 White Pine
5 Poplar
6 Willow
7 Black Walnut
8 Cherry
9 Maple
10 Oak

Using Patterns

Choose one of the patterns from this book based on your interests and your skill level. I have included patterns for 17 projects of different skill levels. To transfer a pattern to the wood, first determine the size you want your carving to be. Copy the pattern on a copy machine, enlarging or reducing the pattern as necessary. If you want to make a carving the same size as those shown in this book, use carbon paper or tracing paper and trace the pattern. Then, use carbon paper to transfer the pattern to

the wood. Or cut out the pattern, lay it on the wood and trace around the cutout. Whichever method you choose, be sure that both the front and side views are lined up properly on the block of wood.

Getting Started

To start, round off the corners of your piece of wood to represent the shape of your carving more closely. If you are unsure what to do after this, refer to your pattern. Sometimes I like to use modeling clay to form an example of what I want to carve, and then I use it to help visualize the designed cuts in a three-dimensional manner.

Below are some tips to help you get started.
• Make cuts clean. Don't keep cutting in the same spot. It will leave knife marks.
• Use gouges to make concave cuts, not a knife.
• To practice carving clean cuts, carve a piece of wood into an egg shape or a round ball.
• Keep knives and gouges sharp enough to cut across the grain.
• Don't try to finish a carving in one sitting.
• Strop your knife frequently while carving. Every 15 minutes is ideal.
• Select a clean, even-grained wood with no knots.
• Layout patterns on the wood so that they are oriented with the grain. If you must extend arms or other part of the carving, it is better to carve them separately and glue them on so they don't cross the grain.
• Seek others' opinions of your work to learn where you may need to improve.
• Practice making eyes on scrap wood before putting them on your carving.
• To dry out green wood, try the microwave oven.
• Draw your ideas in stick form to get action.
• Use clay to form positions and details before carving your project.
• Technique is developed from experience and practice.

Painting Techniques

Before I begin painting a carving, I study a color chart to find an appealing match. For example: If I were using a fire red from the tube, I would mix it with burnt umber for shading in the low areas between the arms and legs and highlight with a lighter white-tone.

I usually paint with artist's oil paints. Oils dry slow and allow me to blend colors easier. I don't put the paint on heavy or thick. I thin it out so that it resembles a stain. Thick paint tends to cover the knife marks that lend character to a piece. If the color is not dark enough, I paint over it again. To finish, I use a satin varnish, and when the carving is dry, I sometimes use a burnt umber wash for a shaded effect.

Acrylics also work well on woodcarvings. I use acrylics when I have to complete a job quickly. Acrylics dry faster than oil paints, and I can speed drying time even more by using a hair dryer between coats.

Sometimes I choose to use a coat of gesso under the paint. The gesso helps to cover up imperfections in the wood. Also, it seems to make the painting show more highlights on the high spots.

Once I've decided on a color scheme and the types of paint I want to use, I'm ready to paint. When using oil colors, I first mix a flesh color and paint the face, hands and legs. While the flesh paint is still wet, I stipple a small amount of red on the face and hands for a ruddy effect. I paint the lips with a darker color plus a cadmium red deep hue. I use a touch of cobalt siccative drier, turpentine and linseed oil with my paint.

After painting the carving, I mix burnt umber with each color and use the new colors to shade all the low spots. Then I use a slight amount of white to stipple the high spots. To paint hair, I keep the paint thin to make the colors as natural as possible and stipple highlights.

Unless I'm blending colors, I let each color dry thoroughly before using the next color. This way I don't smear the paint. When the face is finished and dry, I then do the eyes. First I use white for the eyeball. I chose a color for the iris while the white paint is drying. When the white paint is dry, I paint in the iris. I paint in the pupil and then spot it with a pin dot of white, a bit off center, to highlight the eye.

Step-by-Step

• I use mostly no. 9 or no. 10 gouges. These allow me the versatility of making deep cuts as well as shallow ones.

• I like diamond sharpening stones since they are more aggressive and time saving. I also use a machinist's stone.

• I try to use clear white basswood instead of the darker colored basswood.

• I strop my tools frequently, as often as every 15 minutes.

• A good pencil to use on wood is HB.

• A little oil on the leather strop helps to keep the buffing compound on the leather.

• I use carved pieces of basswood that match the inside profiles of my carving tools. I cover the wood with buffing compound to hone and polish my gouges and V tools.

1 I sketch in the three parts of the face.

2 I start carving the nose using a stop cut at the top and bottom of the nose. I use a knife and a no. 9 - 3mm gouge to cut the eye sockets and sides of nose.

3 Using a no. 9 - 10mm V tool, I rough out the facial features, referring to the pattern frequently. Also, I sketch in guidelines for reference.

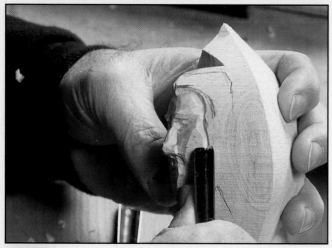

4 I outline the face using the same no. 9 - 10mm V tool.

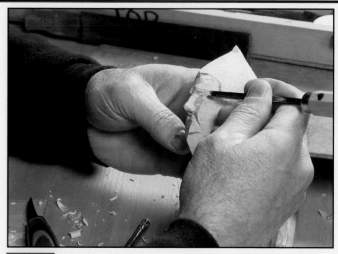

5 Again with the 4mm gouge, I carve the eye sockets creating a mound (football shape) and begin to form the profile.
Note: "Time to strop tools."

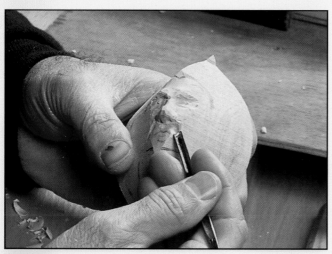

6 Using a no.9 - 4mm gouge, rough out the mouth area.

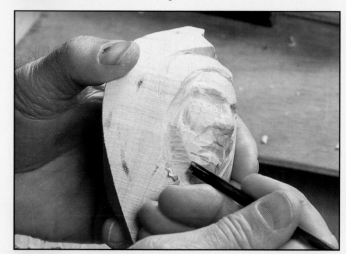

7 With the same gouge, I shape the side of the face, cheek and chin.

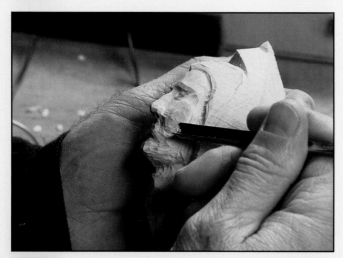

8 When shaping the side of the face, I find that small cuts are better. You don't want to remove too much wood at one time.

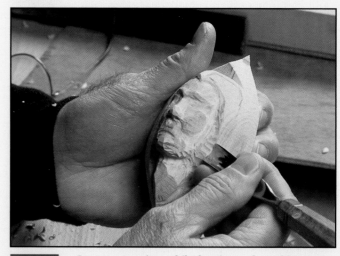

9 I vary gouge sizes while forming and roughing out the facial features. Here a 10mm gouge is being used.

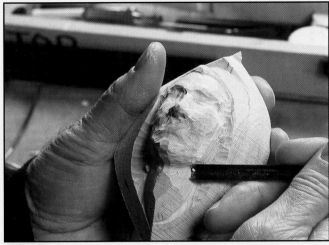

10 Next form the chin and neckline. As I carve each feature, I refer to the pattern and try to make the carving look like the sketch as much as possible. Note: "Time to strop tools."

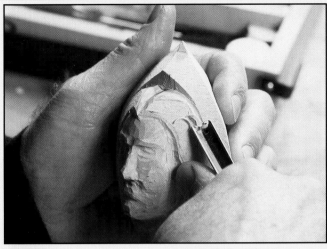

11 When carving hair, start with a large gouge, using wavy cuts. Then go over the area again with smaller gouges (10, 6, 4 and 2 mm in size). This gives the appearance of hair looking more realistic.

12 Next shape the mouth with a 1/2 in. palm gouge.

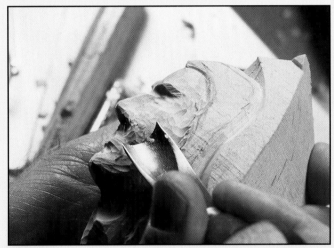

13 Using the same palm gouge, shape the cheeks. The large palm gouge allows you to smooth off the surface.

14 This view shows the bottom of the chin and neck area. I continue using the 1/2 in. palm gouge, making small cuts.

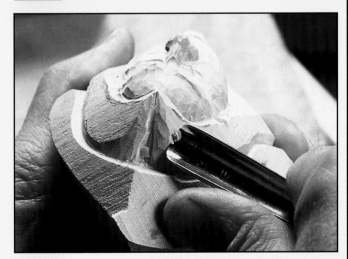

15 Here I put the part in the hair using the palm gouge.

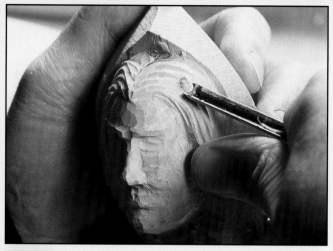

16 4mm gouge working the hairlines: when using gouges, it helps to keep my thumb on the wood for better control.

17 At this point, roughing out the head is nearly complete.

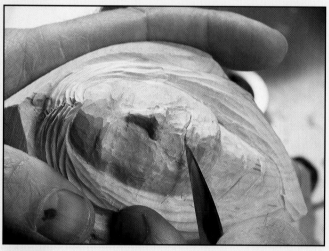

18 After locating the position of the lips, I mark the lines with a pencil. I then make a cut with my knife along the center of the mouth, being careful not to chip the wood.

19 Using a small V palm tool, I clean up the groove between the upper and lower lips.

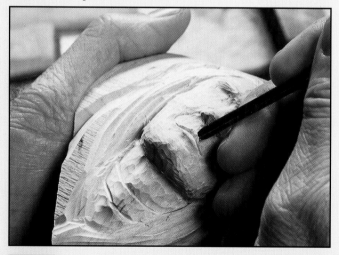

20 With a 3mm gouge, I work on the area under the nose and above the upper lip.
Note: "Time to strop tools."

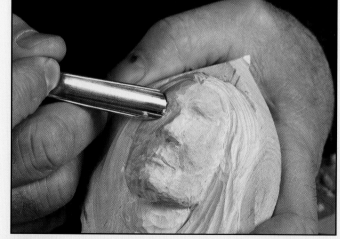

21 Using a 10mm gouge, I refine the facial details, cheeks, nose and chin. I make very small cuts to smooth the face.

22 At this stage, the face and neck have been smoothed.

23 Now pencil in the eyes. When carving faces, I advise carvers to do the eye on the left side first if they are right handed, and the eye on the right first if left handed. Being right handed, I can match the left eye without my hand blocking my view of the eye.

24 Using a very sharp, pointed knife, I make a V cut in the corners of the eyes.

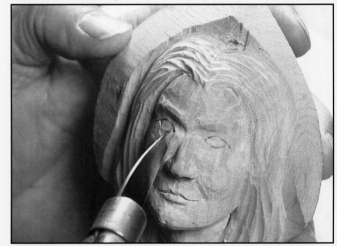

25 I lift out the corner pieces with the knife point, then shape the eyeballs with the knife, being careful not to chip the lids.

26 Using a 2mm palm gouge, I create the upper and lower eyelids.

27 Now check on how the left and right eyes match each other.

 28 I use a 1mm micro gouge to create the pupils. The hair was detailed with flowing lines using a 2mm gouge.

29 I create the neck band with a small V tool.

30 The completed carving ready for painting or varnishing.

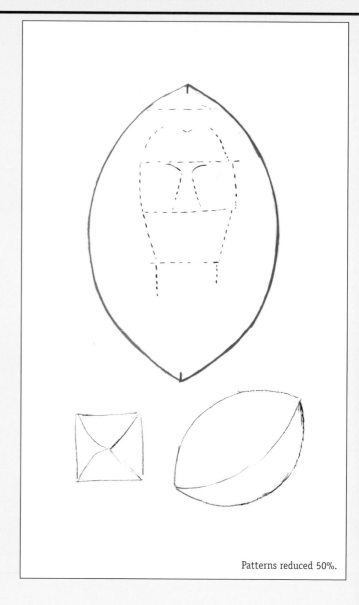

Patterns reduced 50%.

Patterns reduced 50%.

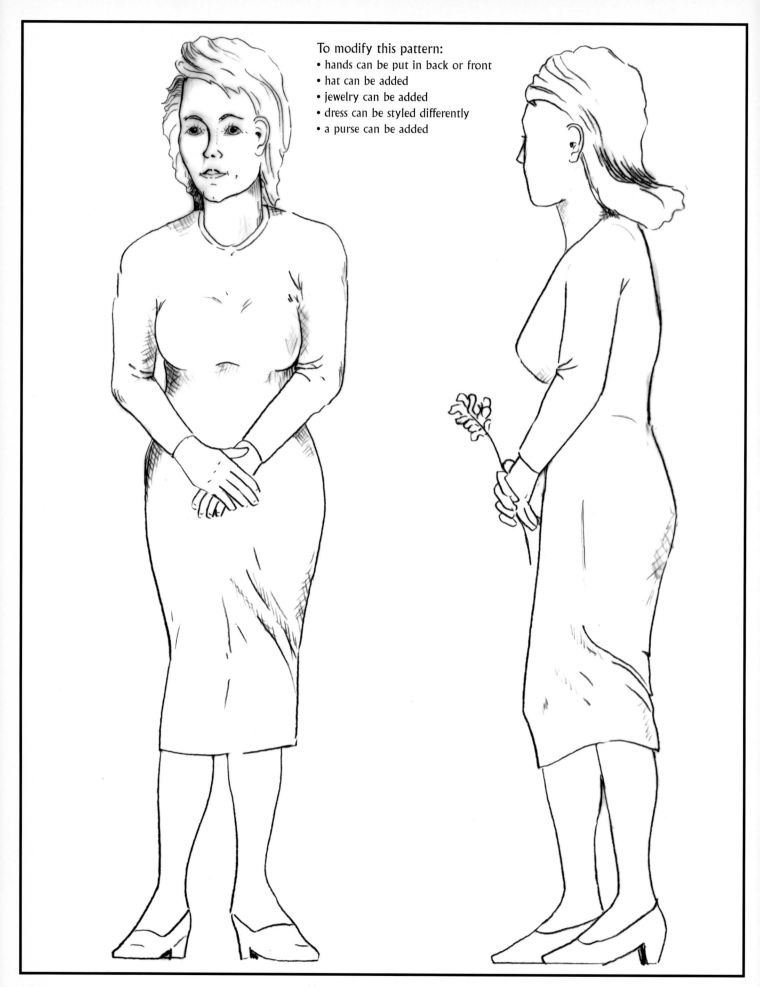

To modify this pattern:
• hands can be put in back or front
• hat can be added
• jewelry can be added
• dress can be styled differently
• a purse can be added

Note: The gun was carved separately and inserted into the hands. The gun pattern here can be used to create the gun.

To modify this pattern:
• change the hat to a plain coon-skin type or remove it
• carve the knapsack and other accessories separately and lay them at his feet or glue them on
• delete the fringes on the coat
• try a different pose with the gun
• add some game (a rabbit or pheasant) to the carving
• carve a beaver trap

Enlarge 110%

R. Oar ©

Enlarge 110%

I came up with the idea for this pattern while shooting at a black powder firing range. A friend of mine—a real mountain man we call Smoking Joe—had this wolf hat on. I thought it would be a neat carving, so I sketched it and later made the pattern and carving.

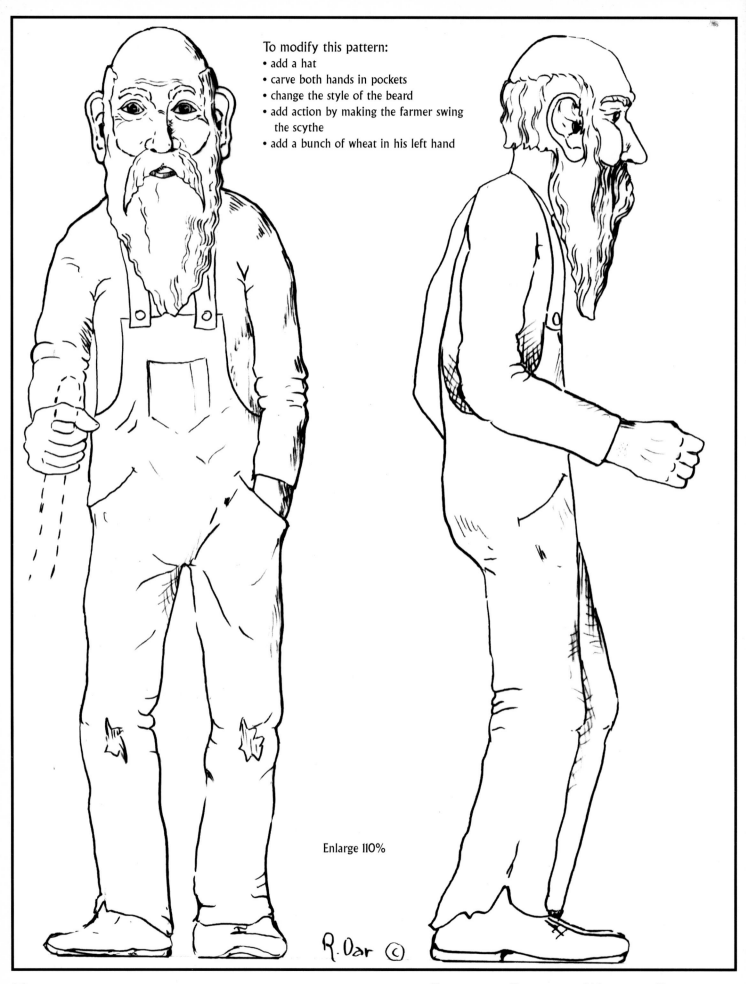

To modify this pattern:
• add a hat
• carve both hands in pockets
• change the style of the beard
• add action by making the farmer swing the scythe
• add a bunch of wheat in his left hand

Enlarge 110%

R. Oar ©

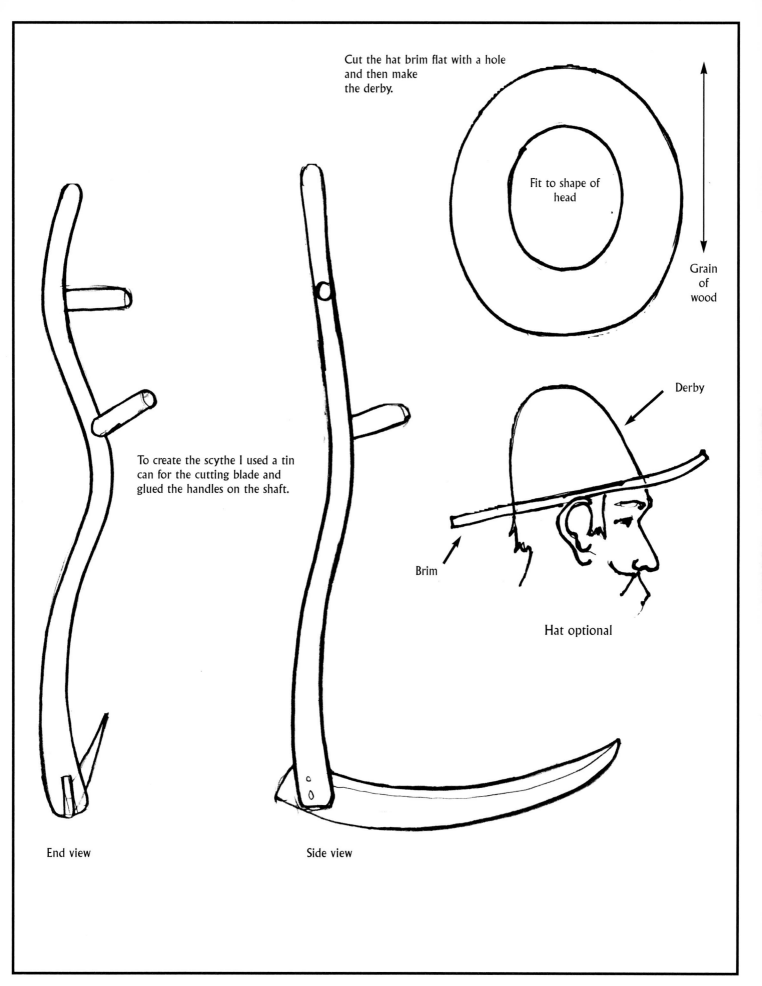

Cut the hat brim flat with a hole and then make the derby.

Fit to shape of head

Grain of wood

Derby

Brim

Hat optional

To create the scythe I used a tin can for the cutting blade and glued the handles on the shaft.

End view

Side view

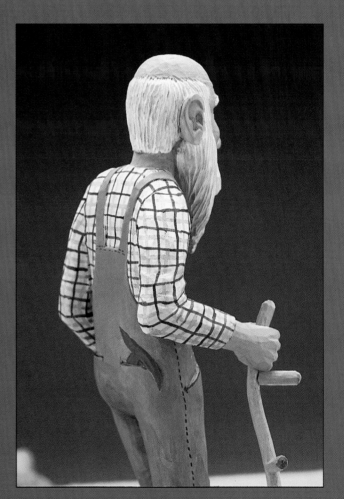

End view of
right arm

The arms are added after carving the
body. A base can be added later.

To modify this pattern:
• carve the hands beside the body
• use a costume without a scarf or other
  extras

Enlarge 105%

R. Oar
©

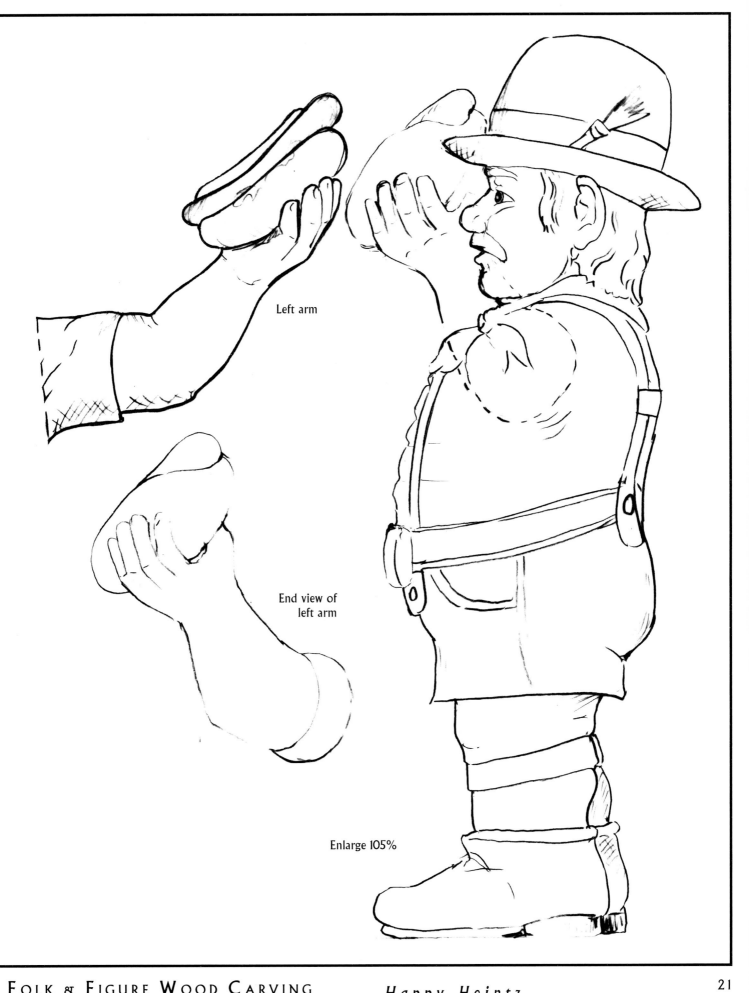

Left arm

End view of
left arm

Enlarge 105%

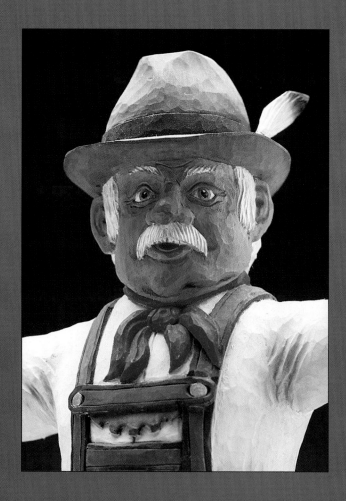

A trip to Germany took us to a costume festival where I came up with the idea for this carving. Folks dressed in traditional costumes are always good inspiration for carvings.

To modify this pattern:
- carve just the figure without the bagpipes and ornamentation
- carve the bagpipes separately and glue them on
- carve a kilt without pleats

Enlarge 115%

R. Oar ©

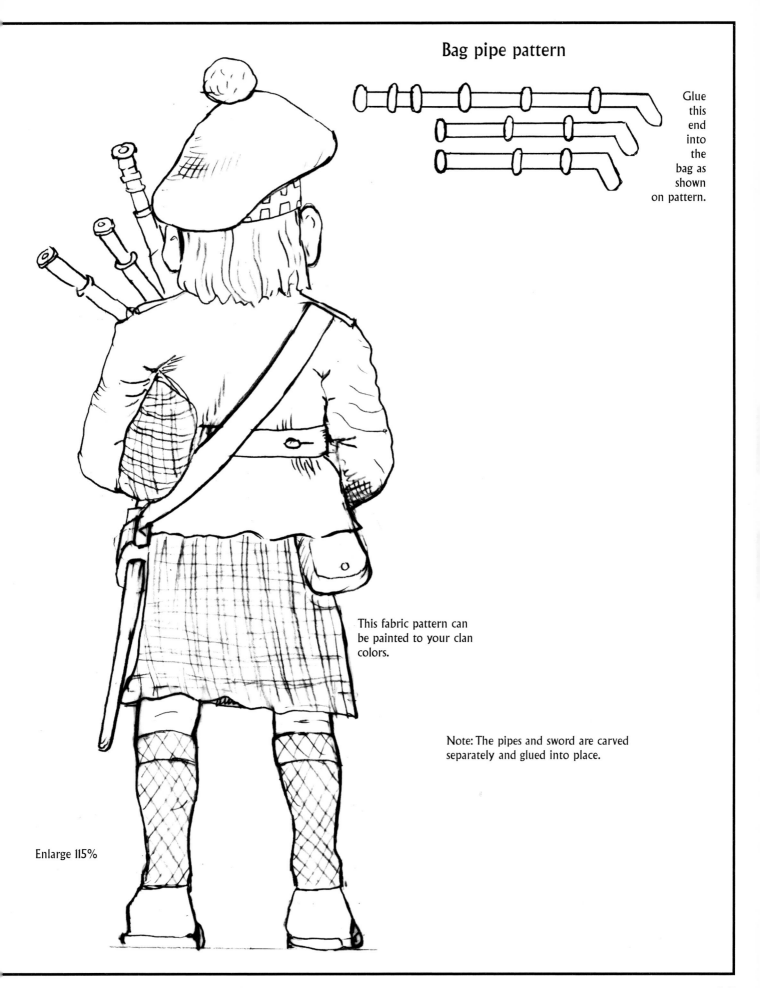

Bag pipe pattern

Glue this end into the bag as shown on pattern.

This fabric pattern can be painted to your clan colors.

Note: The pipes and sword are carved separately and glued into place.

Enlarge 115%

I got my inspiration for this carving from my ancestry. My first name, Ross, was my grandmother's maiden name. Her father was a ship builder from Scotland. And I always liked to hear the bagpipes playing.

To modify this pattern:
- carve both hands on hips
- make the right leg straight
- change the headdress style to include fewer feathers
- replace the spear with a hatchet or your own creation
- add a beaded design to the costume

Enlarge 125%

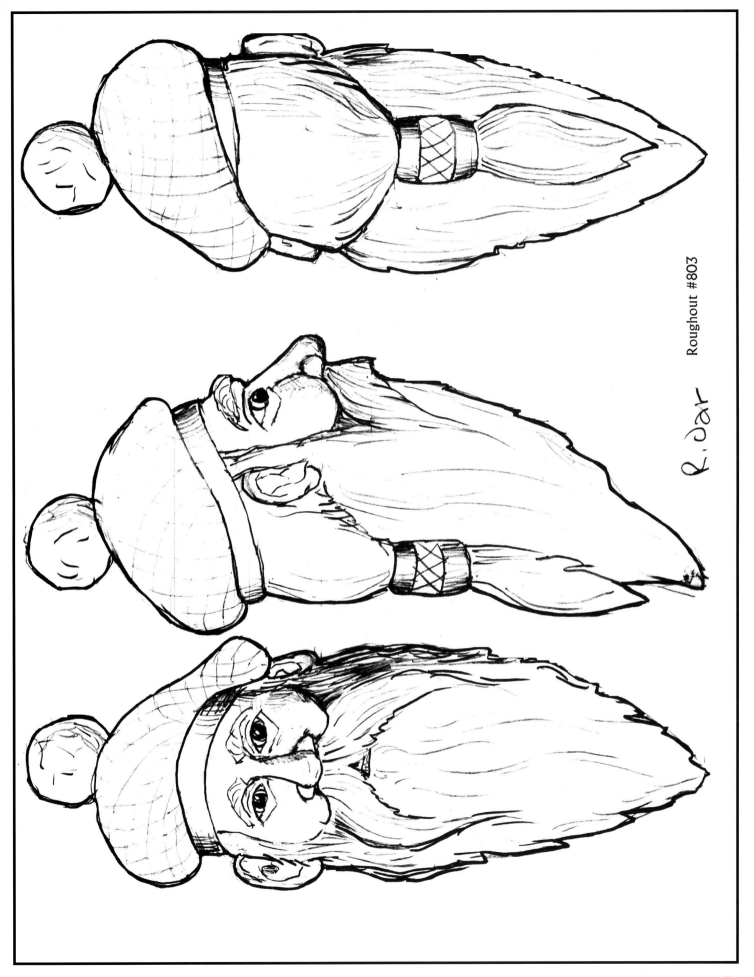

Roughout #803

R. Jar

You can hang this carved head or make a stand for it. Remember to carve the beard and hair in a waving motion to make them look more realistic. His beret can be *green* for Irish or *red* for Scottish.

The name—and the inspiration—for this carving was again pulled from my family ancestry. Dallas was my great great grandfather's name.

Alex the Clown

Family members provide me with endless inspiration. This clown was created for our special grandson #2.

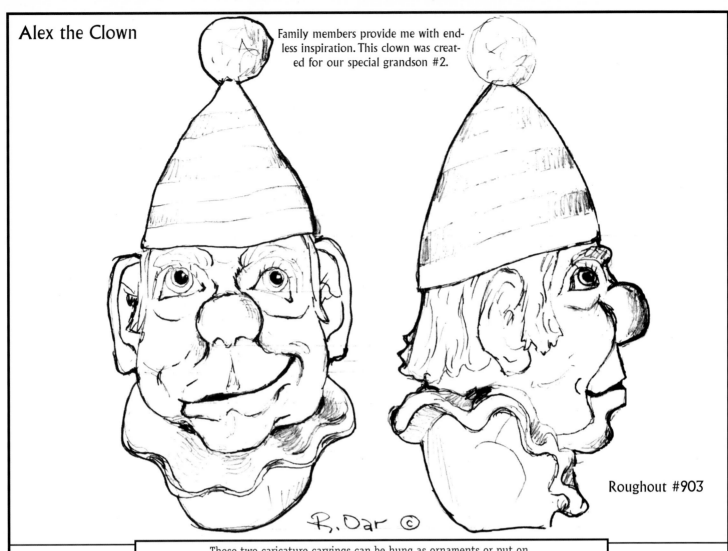

Roughout #903

R. Oar ©

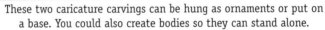

These two caricature carvings can be hung as ornaments or put on a base. You could also create bodies so they can stand alone.

Harley Right

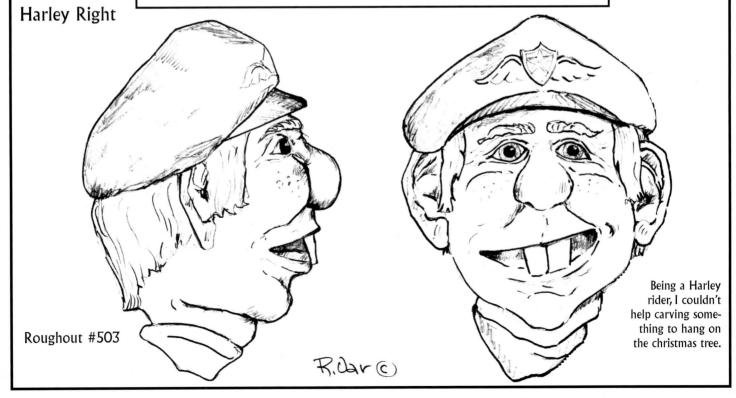

Roughout #503

Being a Harley rider, I couldn't help carving something to hang on the christmas tree.

R. Oar ©

To modify this pattern:
- do not carve holes in the shoes
- give the figure a close-lipped smile
- put both hands in his pockets

Roughout #103

Once again, family provided inspiration for a carving. Though he'll tell you this carving looks nothing like him, our grandson Nathanial was the inspiration behind this carving.

Milly "The City Mouse"— Living in the city she eats well and dresses well, unlike her country cousins.

Note: This body can accommodate other animal heads.

Roughout #603

R. Daw©

Give the Graduate a hat by adding a flat top piece after
the carving is completed. Or carve the hat and the head
together, if you choose.

R. Dar ©

To add a diploma, drill a hole in the
hand and insert the diploma. Or carve the diploma and
the hand together.

Roughout #203

This is a fun first project. It requires a small piece of wood. The thought came to me as I was sitting at the dentist's office.

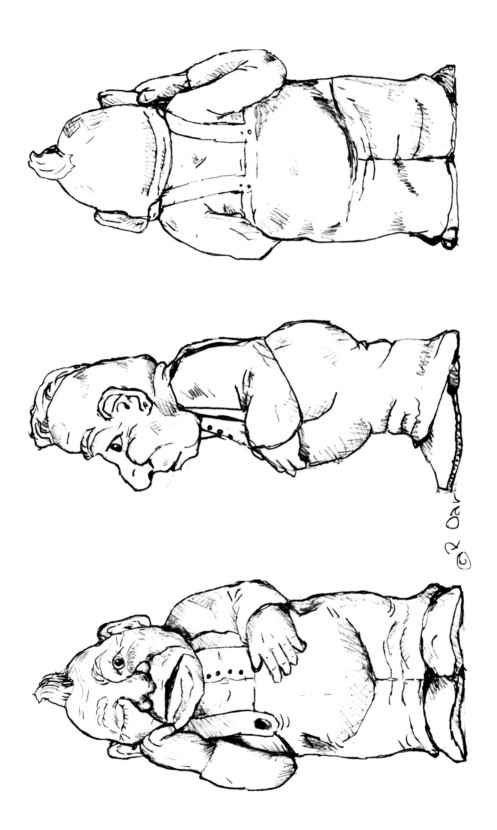

Roughout #303

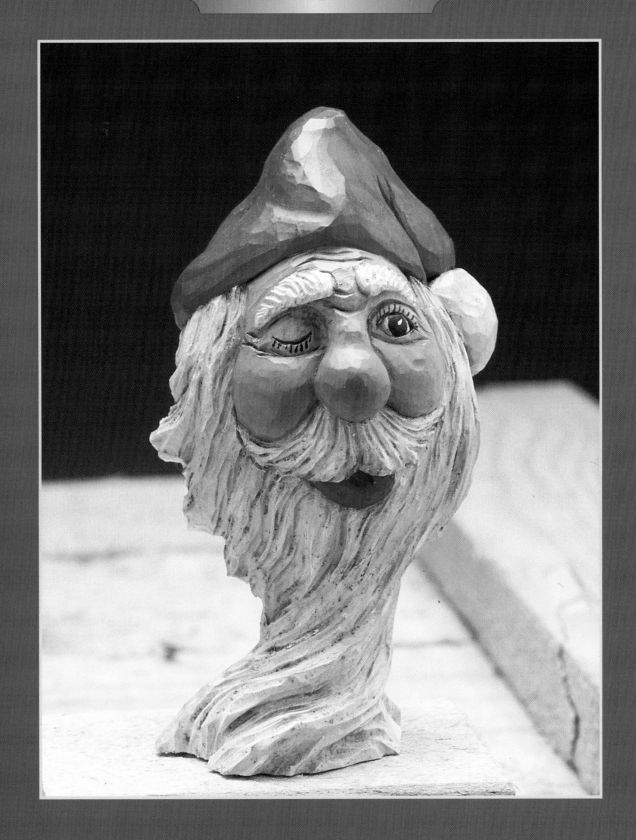

R.Dar ©

This pattern can be done with or without the flowing
beard base. It can also be made as a hanging ornament.

Roughout #703

Wood
Grain

Santa's Sleigh

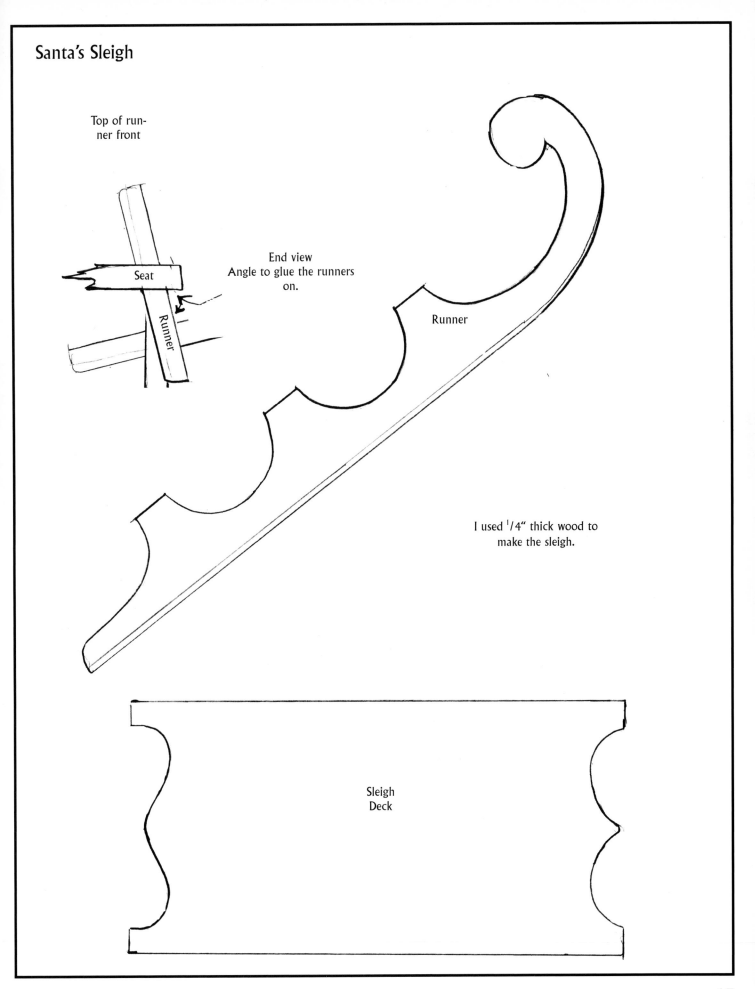

Top of runner front

End view
Angle to glue the runners on.

Seat

Runner

Runner

I used ¹/4" thick wood to make the sleigh.

Sleigh Deck

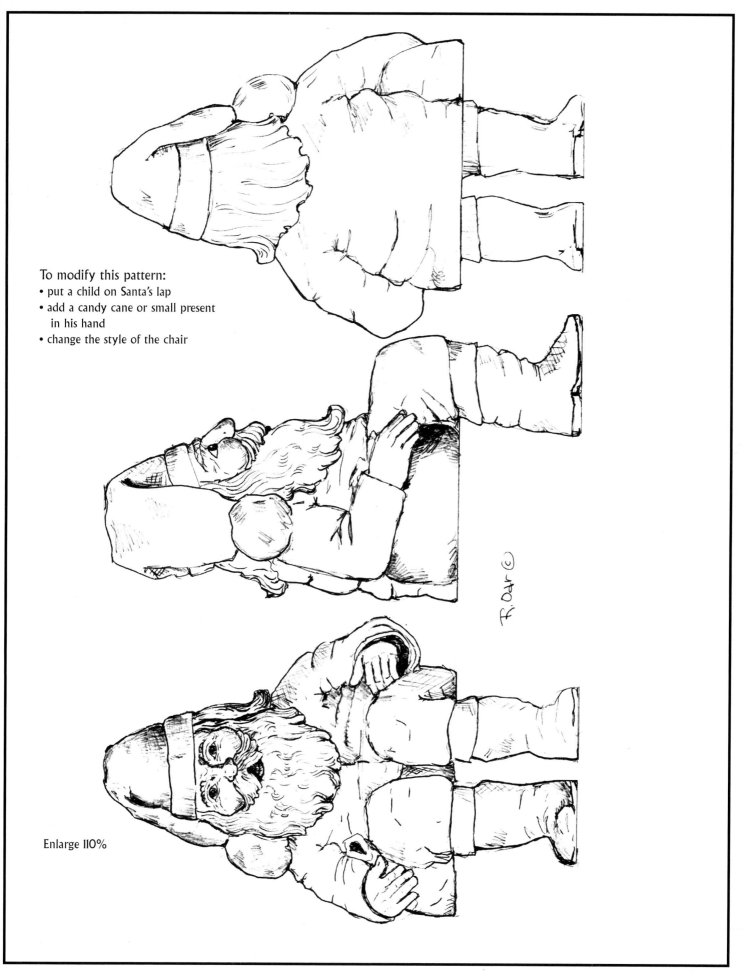

To modify this pattern:
- put a child on Santa's lap
- add a candy cane or small present in his hand
- change the style of the chair

F. Dyer ©

Enlarge 110%

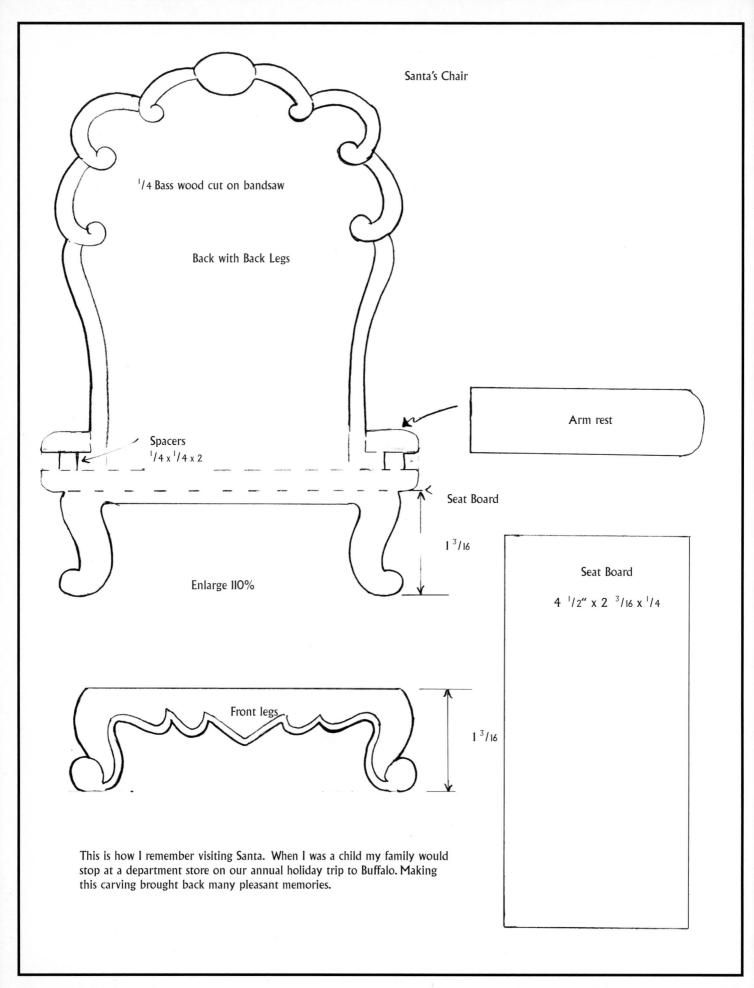

Santa's Chair

1/4 Bass wood cut on bandsaw

Back with Back Legs

Arm rest

Spacers
1/4 x 1/4 x 2

Seat Board

1 3/16

Enlarge 110%

Seat Board

4 1/2" x 2 3/16 x 1/4

Front legs

1 3/16

This is how I remember visiting Santa. When I was a child my family would stop at a department store on our annual holiday trip to Buffalo. Making this carving brought back many pleasant memories.